THE FIVE FOLD WORK OF THE EVANGELIST

God's Church Administration

Luis R. Lugo, M.Th.

Published by:
L&L Publication
1301 Poplar Court
Homewood, IL 60430

DEDICATION

To my wife, Andrea of 33 years, whose support, encouragement, sacrifice and toil has allowed me to pursue the task of being God's church administrator! With all of my love and appreciation, I dedicate this book to you!

SPECIAL THANKS

Special thanks to Dr. James Maxwell for his many suggestions and corrections of this manuscript and for his encouragement in this work. Also special thanks to Bro. J. S. Winston, Dean of Preachers, for his encouragement and suggestions in the publishing of this manuscript. Also to Sister Yvonne Wyatt for her help in suggestions and corrections. Special thanks to Sister Michelle Byrd and Angela Wright for her typing and retyping of the manuscript and making all corrections necessary.

Thanks to Ralston Mondaize for his critical review and suggestions! And to Dr. W. F. Washington for his observations and encouragement.

TABLE OF CONTENTS

INTRODUCTION

U nder the influence and inspiration of the Holy Spirit, Paul encouraged young Timothy, whom he had left at Ephesus, "to do the work of the Evangelist" (**2 Tim. 4:5**) (**Eph. 4:1**).

From the very inception of the Christian dispensation, the work of the Evangelist has been a source of much conjecture. And, even today this conjecture still lingers on. Was his work a continuous one? Or is his work like that of the apostles and prophets, in that once served they are no longer necessary? Is there reallly a need for an evangelist in a local congregation that has duly ordained elders and deacons? If so what is the role of the evangelist? These and other questions must be answered if the church is to have a proper understanding of the role and place of the evangelist in the local congregation.

The word "work" in our text means a laborer, an employee, one who performs a deed. Every Christian according to Paul is on God's payroll (**Eph. 4:1**). But the evangelist is uniquely employed to do a specific work. He is on God's payroll and he is directly responsible to God to perform certain functions.

An evangelist is one who heralds, proclaims or brings the good news of the salvation offered by God in Christ to the world. The evangelist is described by the Greek word (Keruso) which means one who proclaims one who sets forth an announcement. In this instance the evangelist is like the old town crier that announces what time of day or night it is. Only in this instance he announces the (Kerygma) or the substance of God's message.

But is this all there is to being an evangelist? From the most highly held opinions it would seem that way. But when Paul told Timothy to do "the work of the evangelist," Paul gave us a different picture of the work and nature of the job.

The work of the evangelist as outlined by Paul in the books of **I and II Timothy** and **Titus** gives us an overall view of the diverse work of this person. In trying to put in capsule form the work of the evangelist, I believe that we can put them under these headings:

1. **Proclaimer – That is, he is to preach, herald proclaim the gospel (2 Tim. 4:1-8)**

2. **Trainer – He is to train the local church (2 Tim. 2:2; Tit. 2)**

3. **Organizer – He is to "set in order the things that are lacking" (Tit. 1:5)**

4. **Defender** – He is to be set for the defense of the gospel, his most ardent task (2 Tim. 1:13)
5. **Discipliner** – (Tit. 3:10)

This work calls for men of unique qualifications as well as love for God, His Word, church and lost mankind. It calls for men of unique faith as well as resounding confidence in the task entrusted them by God. It calls for men of discipline and commitment that transcends ordinary Christian services!

The Role of the Evangelist in the Scheme of Redemption, the Church and Society

The evangelist is a vital cog in the scheme of God's redemption. The scheme of redemption is God's plan of salvation. The role of the evangelist must not be downplayed because of one's misunderstandings and misconceptions as to what God thinks of him. His place in that scheme is seen in **Eph. 4:11-16:**

"And he gave to some to be apostles, and some prophets and **evangelist**, and some pastors and teachers for the perfecting of the saints, unto the work of the ministry unto the building up of the body of Christ; till we all attain unto the unity of the faith, and of the knowledge of the Son of God, unto a full grown man, unto measure of the stature of the fullness of Christ: that we may be no longer children tossed to and fro and carried about with every wind of doctrine, by the slight of men, in craftiness, after the wiles of the error; but speaking the truth in love, may grow up in all things unto him, who is the head even Christ, from whom all the body fitly framed and knit together that which every joint supplieth, according to the working in due measure of each several part, making the increase of the body unto the building up of itself in love."

Again, in **Romans 10:13-15**:

"for whosover shall call upon the name of the Lord shall be saved. How then shall they call on him in whom they have not heard? And how shall they hear without a preacher? And how shall they preach, except they be sent? Even as it is written, how beautiful are the feet of them that bring glad tidings of good things."

Paul shows us several things from these verses in regard to the role of the evangelist in God's scheme of redemption and in relation to the church.

It is evident from these two passages of scriptures that the evangelist is more than just a bringer of "good tidings," but that his function is indispensable in the universal salvation of the lost and the nurture of the local church! This also serves to separate the notion that anyone can be an evangelist just because he can put a lesson or two together for delivery on certain occasions. Beloved, there is more to the work of the evangelist than just preparing a lesson for delivery.

Also, one sees his role in the invaluable services he performs in the administration of carrying out his role. Who receives the call when there is death or illness or some crisis in the home? Who serves as counselor, referee, civic leader, performs weddings and funerals? Whom does the community see as someone you can trust, look up to and rely on? Who brings more degradation and shame when he is caught in uncompromising situations? The evangelist.

The evangelist is seen as a spokesman not only for God, but also for the underprivileged, the downtrodden and the oppressed. Evangelists have been thrown into the limelight of civil rights, politics, education, fundraising, protesting, leading marches against discrimination. Evangelists are seen as frontrunners in the fight against pornography, abortion and sex education.

Thus, the evangelist occupies a unique role as it relates to the scheme of redemption, the maturing of the church, and a godly influence in the world.

Misconceptions That Are Prevalent Today Concerning the Evangelist

What is an evangelist?

We have already said that he was a Proclaimer, a heralder of the good tidings of the good news. But there is a grave misconception of what his true function is.

That the evangelist is a pastor, bishop, overseer, shepherd, presbyter, or elder. The Scriptures teach that there are distinctive officers in the local church. The term church means the "Called out, assembly, congregation". It is described as the body of Christ (**Col. 1:18; Eph. 1:22-23; I Cor. 12:13**).

The Church is seen in two senses:

- The universal church is composed of baptized believers throughout the history of man from its inception (**Matt. 16:18**).

- The local church is composed of baptized believers in a local geographical area such as the church at Ephesus (**Eph. 1:1-2**) or the church of Corinth (**I Cor. 1:1-2**).

It is within the local church that God has placed these distinctive officers. And there is a distinctive difference between an evangelist as described in the Bible and what the religious world calls a pastor, bishop or evangelist.

The Bible plainly speaks of evangelists and pastors as separate church officials. In the first century when there were no
existing denominations, the evangelist was one thing and the
pastor was another. In **I Tim. 3:1-8**, Paul speaks of the office
of the elder. He lists the qualifications, both positive and negative.

These qualifications were for men who along with the
evangelist served in the maturing process of the local congregation. These qualifications clearly point out that pastors were
to be men of "age, wisdom, and stability; men who by reason
of time have been exercised in the spiritual development of the
divine nature", and who knew the local church and understood its human nature.

It was the responsibility of the evangelist to ordain these
men in the local church, (**Tit. 1:5**) to rebuke them publicly
when they receive an accusation that was provable against
them, (**I Tim. 5:3,2**), and to see to it that the church honored
elders who were "worthy of double honor" (**I Tim. 5:20**).

But today the evangelist in the church has assumed the
duties and responsibilities of the pastor while his true work by
and large suffers and in most cases goes undone with the
results that the local church suffers and his office is minimized!
It is therefore encumbered upon serious men who understand
the plain teaching of the Bible, to show from the scriptures
that the evangelist is not a pastor, not an errand boy, a

Corporate Board Executive, but that he is to be respected, loved, esteemed and supported as he discharges his God-given responsibilities.

The local church must realize that the evangelist is a spokesman for God! He is employed by God and he has authority by the very fact that he has been ordained to preach the Gospel, train the church, set it in order whenever things are lacking, win souls and defend the faith from heretical attacks from perverters of the truth.

To those who aspire to proclaim the Gospel, remember to be an evangelist. As a successful evangelist, you must know what the work is. There must be the resolve to see that work through. That there are hardships to endure, difficulties encountered and more than likely the storm and wrath of those who are worldly minded, both within the church and out of the church. And that success must not be measured in the number of members, but in the free course of God's word in the lives of people, and that he can proclaim the word freely and without doubt or fear of mankind!

SECTION ONE

The Preaching of the Gospel

Is a picture worth a thousand words?

Someone has said, "a picture is worth a thousand words." It sounds good, but who can paint a picture of Jefferson's "Declaration of Independence", or Abraham Lincoln's "Gettysburg Address", or Patrick Henry's "Give Me Liberty or Give Me Death" speech? What painting ever portrayed a truer picture of the dream of the American Negro than Martin Luther King's "I Have a Dream" speech, or for that matter, Jesse Jackson's speech at the Democratic National Convention?

What picture has ever had the impact on the lives of people down through the centuries like the words of Jesus recorded in Matthew, Chapters 5 through 7? Or the sermon of Peter on Pentecost when people who helped put the nails in the hands of Christ cried out in repentance, "…what shall we do?"

What picture could describe the lives of humble evangelists going from town to town with simplicity of speech, yet turning cities upside down as men and women responded to their proclamation of God's word?

What picture could describe the impact that the preaching of men like Wycliffe, Martin Luther and John Huss had on the lives of those in the Dark Ages?

What picture ever freed slaves, elevated downtrodden womanhood and brought peace to a world full of unrest? What picture ever took a drunk out of a gutter and made a respectable man out of him? What picture ever started schools, hospitals, and human treatment for the downcast and downtrodden?

The quotation might sound good, but the faithful proclamation of an evangelist will have more impact than any picture Michelangelo, or for that matter, any of the world's renowned artists could paint.

When we speak of the work of the evangelist we are setting forth what God considers his function to be. Therefore, as we look at the work of the evangelist we list as the first and primary function, the proclamation of the death, burial and resurrection of Jesus Christ for the remission of sins (**I Cor. 15:1-4**).

What is preaching?

Preaching is not mere story telling or performing for the entertainment of an audience, but rather it is relating how the historical life of the Son of God affects one's life both physically and spiritually. It is how that through the crucifixion, death, burial and the resurrection of an itinerant preacher one can find freedom from sin and its eternal consequences. It is how that those who are alienated from God, strangers to the covenant of promise, can have a right relationship through an obedient faith.

Avenue of Reconciliation

In the preaching of the Gospel, the evangelist presents the "power of God" (**Rom. 1:16**). Here Paul conveys his feeling that he is "not ashamed of the gospel" because it is God's ultimate power to save the lost! Herein lies the necessity of preaching. It is done in order to save or rescue the lost from his destiny with Hell.

Preaching is the avenue by which the power of God is transmitted to those who are in sin and in need of restoration, rejuvenation, reconciliation, and reconstruction (**I Cor. 1:21**).

Relating the Ongoing Historical Narrative

Preaching is relating the ongoing historical narrative of God's redemptive plan. It is the sharing of that which energizes the downtrodden, rekindles the fires of hope, which have gone out. It influences the heart of man to strive for the calling of the high purpose of God in Christ. It brings about the desires of the heart to be submissive to a loving and tender father, who cares much more for us than we will ever learn to care for each other. It is in the retelling of that ongoing experience that there is hope for the hopeless, sight for the blind, strength for the weak, and help for the helpless. It is the soothing of the pain of sin and how God is willing and able to take our sins away and forgive mankind for his offenses. It is this ongoing relationship that man must seek to reach and it is in this event that the evangelist finds his most effective results, as he relates the word of God to the dilemmas that face mankind daily! It is in this event that the evangelist must be at his best yet his humblest, totally prepared yet knowing he does not really know enough. He is wise, yet not with the wisdom of the world.

It is in this phase that the evangelist must heed the warning and admonition of Paul, "preach the word" (**2 Tim. 4:2**). It is no time for speculations, prognostications, spectacularism or showmanship. But rather it is a time to speak that which "befits sound doctrine" (Tit. 2:1). It is a time to stay within "the doctrine of Christ" (**2 John 9-11**).

Heralding the Word

By "speaking as the oracles of God" (**I Pet. 4:15**), it is a time "not to go beyond the things which are written" (**I Cor. 4:6**), it is to speak as if one's vocal cords had been touched by the hand of God and words were placed there by the majestic mind of the creator! Yes, preaching is the presentation of God's inspired word in an inspired way. It is the pointing out of God's love for man, therefore, His doctrine needs to be explained, His discipline carried out, His purpose for mankind and His eternal wisdom shared.

Preaching should be the crying out of God's Celestial Truths, not the bombastic explosions of likes and dislikes! All too often, the pew packer is used as a sounding board for one's preconceived ideas and falsified notions or the object of chastisement by an abusive and abrasive volley of verbal insults.

The many negative instructions found in God's word must be presented with a positive approach! The denunciation of sin must be of such a nature that the sinner understands his plight while realizing he can return to God for forgiveness. Yet, so much of the preaching done today is as its best sensationalism linked with a psychological twist and very little substance from God's Word.

Preaching is not the mere employment of mere rhetoric! It is not just the sprouting of verbs, adverbs, and adjectives in rhythmic chant. It is not moaning and groaning and foaming at the mouth. It is not pulsating and yelling or ecstatic outbursts. But rather it is what Haggai did when he was called of

God to speak to the nation of Israel, "then spake Haggai Jehovah's messenger in Jehovah's message" (**Haggai 1:13**).

Declaring the Whole Counsel of God

Preaching is declaring the "whole counsel of God" and not just some favorite portion of it. There are areas that are liked and disliked and areas hard to be understood. There are areas that call for all night research, meditation, prayer and agony, as well as areas of controversy and hot issues that call for a declarative stand.

Proclaiming the Righteousness of God

Preaching is declaring the "righteousness of God." It is a call for purity in the lives of the hearers. It is the cleansing agent of God to help man wash and keep sins away. It is the declaration that the God of the universe is a righteous God and hates every evil way! Preaching is showing that the God of the Bible is a God of ethical and moral righteousness as well as religious righteousness, that He cares for the individual as well as the masses; that He expects all levels of righteousness from those who profess faith in Him.

Declaring the Grace of God

Preaching is declaring the "grace of God" as it teaches men how to "deny ungodliness and worldly lust", that we can live "soberly, righteously and godly in this present world" (**Tit. 2:11-13**).

Things Needed to Preach

There is more to preaching than stabbing someone with the pointed sword of God's Word. It is the ability to kill the sin while saving the sinner. This, then is the evangelist's greatest task. Yet, it is precisely here that many evangelists fail. Why? Because they do not create the right type of study habits that make them fresh and interesting while telling the same old story.

Many have the erroneous view that all they have to do is open their mouths and the Spirit of God will put words there. While they have not had any contact with the tool of the Spirit which is the Word of God (**Eph. 6:18**).

It must be understood that in order for an evangelist to preach God's glory effectively, he must spend time in:

- Study (**2 Tim. 2:15**)
- Mediation (**Ps. 1**)
- Prayer (**Acts 6:4**)
- Contact with people (**I Tim. 4:12-16**)

In study, it will call for an adequate and extensive library, where the proper research can be done. A place where the evangelist can meditate upon the things which he has studied and pray for wisdom, understanding and the ability to dispense God's Word to those who need it.

A pitfall that the evangelist must also avoid is not to ever use the preaching of the Gospel to pontificate about problems, which he has, thinking that because he has them everyone else has them! This is not to say that he should not share his problems with the congregation and how the Lord has helped him to overcome. This indeed would help the Church see the struggling human side of the evangelist. But he should not allow the pulpit to become his personal platform to dump all of his problems on the congregation! A systemic and disciplined study habit, coupled with meditation and prayer as well as contact with people, will go a long way to help solve this problem. Also, it will help the Church to see spiritual growth in the life of the evangelist as well as in the lives of the members.

One thing all evangelists of the Gospel must remember is that the preparation of lessons takes time and that a misuse of time will cause an improper presentation both in delivery, context and understanding.

Ministering to the Needs of the People

The second thing that the evangelist must realize is that as he heralds the good news, he is also ministering to the needs of his listeners. There are those who make a distinction between an evangelist and a minister. The popular notion is that the evangelist is one who proclaims the death, burial, and resurrection of Jesus Christ as a traveling messenger, while a minister administers, guides and pastors a local body.

In the biblical sense it is impossible to minister without evangelizing and to evangelize without ministering, for neither of these are ever completed. Evangelism is an ongoing process by which a person is brought to a right relationship with God and is set free through the ministry of the Word.

The reason God gave the distinctive offices to the Church (Eph. 4:11) was for the maturing process. The evangelist is part of that process, and this would be incomplete if he failed to meet the needs of his hearers. It is here that the evangelist ministers! It is here that we see him at his true character, a servant. A servant not only of God but also of the Church. Yet, it is precisely here that many evangelists lose their effectiveness because they do not see themselves as servants, but rather as those who are to be served. The evangelist who does not get caught up in the dilemma of titles, positions, and egotistical malfunctions, but who humbly serves the congregation will be blessed in his ministry by God.

Now some may want to take exception to the fact that an evangelist is a minister. But before they do, they should consider the words of Paul to Timothy **in 2 Timothy 4:5-6**, "…do the work of an evangelist fulfill thy ministry." Paul had not only left Timothy at Ephesus to do the work of the evangelist, but he considered it a ministry as well. Paul told Timothy to minister to the Church protecting it against false teachers (**I Tim. 1:3**). He was to teach the Church how to behave (**I Tim. 3:15**). He was to ordain elders and deacons (**I Tim. 3:1-2**). He was to rebuke disorderly elders (**I Tim. 5:20**) and anyone who went against the sound doctrine. He was to mature the Church as well as to help save the lost (**I Tim. 4:12**).

The notion that an evangelist who travels extensively receives more notoriety can be very misleading. Anyone who can speak can come up with seven or eight good sermons by which he can lift the rafters. But the evangelist who builds a local church to the glory of God does so by ministering to the needs of the church day in and day out, by spending time with the problems of the people he serves and by helping them find solutions, will accomplish more and help more people to be faithful, loyal and obedient to the will of God, than all the globetrotting preachers ever will!

How Should He Preach

In the preaching of the Gospel, how should the evangelist proclaim the message? I believe it was the late Levi Kennedy who said "Either put some fire in your sermon or put your sermon in the fire!" This advice needs to be heeded by many evangelists in our brotherhood!

Too many sermons emanating from our pulpits have no

substance, no cohesion, no purpose, no authority, no creativity, and no depth. Many sermons are mere jargons of colloquial statements, empty rhetoric which may emotionalize but which has no lasting substance or value.

To speak effectively does not mean that emotionalism should be excluded and that scholarship be so profound that the audience is more in tune with scholarship than with the message of God's Word, but rather the evangelist should speak with authority (Tit. 2:15). He should realize that he is speaking for God and that he must "speak as the oracles of God" (I Pet. 4:11). Speaking with authority carries with it the idea of conviction, not mere milquetoast speeches but speeches that are sound in essence, speech that is based on evidence that cannot be refuted. It is a "thus saith the Lord speech." It is a vibrant, living message; it is not some sentimental expression of neo-pacifism. But it is a bold proclamation, yet humble in delivery.

Speaking with authority is not being crude and abrasive; but rather it is a prepared delivery of God's executive orders without addition, subtraction, or personal amendments. Speaking with authority is to speak faithfully the Word of God without using it in a deceitful manner, (2 Cor. 4:2). It is making proper contextual exegesis, in all of its contexts, whether it is remote, immediate or historical. It is making application to the person listening. The one who is speaking with authority is speaking without compromise or patronizing. It is not a "better felt than told experience" but a thorough dealing with the text at hand.

Preaching with authority is not necessarily proclaiming one's convictions. One's convictions may rest on preconceived ideas and personal opinions as well as environmental factors. This is precisely what is wrong with the religious world – too many people preaching their convictions rather than a "Thus saith the Lord."

Authoritative preaching may not be necessarily that which brethren proclaimed or what a group of popular preachers may expound on! Authoritative preaching comes with the ring of genuineness. It comes as a "thus saith the Lord." It is provable and never mere assertion. It is consistent with known and revealed truth, and it is never new. As in the word of Foy E. Wallace, "If it's new, it's not true, and if it's true, it's not new."

In order for the evangelist to preach with authority, he naturally must be an ongoing student of the Word. No evangelist ever arrives! There is always one more verse to memorize, one more book to read, one more problem to solve, one more word of encouragement to give and one more sermon to deliver. He must spend time with God in the vestibules of Heaven. He must be able to walk through the fiery furnaces of afflictions. He must spend some time in the wilderness of desolation where God can fine-tune him.

Every congregation should encourage it's minister to lock himself in the inner chambers of his study, remove the telephone from his office, replenish his library from time to time and tell him not to come forth until he has "an authoritative word from the Lord."

SECTION TWO

Training the Church

In **Ephesians the Word "for" as found in verse 12 quali-
fies 4:11, the distinctive officers given to the Church.**

According to Paul, these distinctive officers were given for:

• The perfecting of the saints
• The work of the ministry
• The building up of the body of Christ

As we look at these goals we find that the functions of the
evangelist is to train the Church to perfection, to bring them
to the point where they can do the work of the ministry and
in turn help build up the body of Christ.

These tasks call for training, instructions, motivation,
guiding, discipline and understanding.

Who then is the evangelist to train?

The evangelist is not under orders to train unfaithful, uncooperative, lazy or indifferent members. Many evangelists find themselves with tremendous problems by training unconverted, unspiritual, unfaithful men for positions that require commitment, spirituality, and unwavering faith in God and His Word.

Faithful men—"and the things which thou hast heard from me among many witnesses the same commit thou to faithful men, who shall be able to teach others also" (**2 Tim. 2:2**).

It is God's design that the evangelist invests his life in the lives of those who exemplify fidelity to God. This person's life is convicted and persuaded that God is. And his life is controlled and guided by the Word of God.

Preachers—Evangelist

This training seems to indicate the training of men to be evangelists. Herein is God's prescription for the ongoing supply of faithful evangelists who shall be able to continue to reproduce men with the ability to teach others also.

Herein is one of the greatest services an evangelist can make to the overall scheme of redemption.

He can take a faithful man and teach him what he himself has been taught by the Word of God. What a tremendous legacy! The seed of one evangelist can effect the lives of generations yet unborn! What a tremendous opportunity afforded by God to an evangelist! However, because of jealousy and the notion of being supplanted, many evangelists are remiss in their God given responsibility of training evangelists.

The best way of overcoming these two factors is doing what Paul said, "train faithful men," and leave the unfaithful alone!

How should these men be trained? It is almost impossible to train someone to be an evangelist without getting involved in the life of that person. Thus one method will be the one-on-one method where the evangelist spends time with the prospect in personal evangelism, prayer, biblical study, character building, and fellowshipping with orders of kindred spirits.

The evangelist should teach the faithful how to respect the authority inherent in God's Word. He should seek to ground and establish them in the faith to the point that he knows they are "steadfast, unmovable and abounding in the work of the Lord" (I Cor. 15:58).

Next, he should teach them to be objective and persistent in their personal study; to be honest and diligent in the search of God's truth, and to realize that there will be those who will not agree with their findings. They should, nevertheless, not be afraid or intimidated by their conclusions if they are based on the honest and diligent study of God's Word.

In this phase of personal Bible study, the trainee should be encouraged to establish his own personal library. Here the experienced evangelist can give a list of books that will help the aspiring evangelist to learn how to research the bible for himself. Also, it should be impressed upon the aspiring evangelist the necessity of record keeping, notekeeping and keeping a record of selective passages of Scripture which should be committed to memory.

As the training goes on, they should be trained to make proper presentations of God's Word and how to teach with visual aids.

A course in public speaking and communications will greatly help the trainee. The trainee should be thoroughly trained to preach, to train, to set in order, to defend the faith and to administer discipline.

The faithful evangelist who trains a faithful brother to train others will find personal satisfaction in dealing with God's people.

The question may be asked, "How do you determine if a man is faithful?" Remember the words of Christ, "By their fruits ye shall know them." A faithful man cannot help but do the things assigned to him by God's Word. Does he study on his own? Is he faithful in his relationship with the Church? Does he understand the basic doctrine of the Scriptures? Does he possess a burning desire to bring others to God? Is he secure in his relationship with God? Is he reliable, accountable, and workable? How does he work with others? Does he have the respect of his family, friends and the community? Can you trust him? These and other questions can only be answered by carefully looking and allowing time to prove or disprove a man's worth. Thus, an evangelist must take his time in analyzing those who possess these traits that eventually will help him to teach others also.

I believe that if every evangelist would take one faithful brother and would dedicate himself to this one function, there would be no real need to send men off to schools of preaching where they would not get that individual teaching under the ideal situations that occur in a daily congregational setting.

Elders

The evangelist is to train faithful men to become elders in the local Church (**Tit. 1:5; I Tim. 3:1-7; 2 Tim.2:2**).

In **I Tim.3:1-7**, Paul gives the qualifications, which are necessary for those men who would help the church to be mature. He begins by pointing out to Timothy that "if a man desires the office of a bishop or overseer, he desires a good work." Here is one of the keys to being a successful evangelist, the ability to bring a man to the desire of wanting to be an overseer in the local church. A local congregation is composed of baptized believers.

The function of the elders differs from the evangelist in their realm of work. When we look at the functions of elders we find that their primary function are these:

- Watching (**Acts 20:28-31**)
- Admonishing (**2 Thess. 3:6-15**)
- Feeding and tending the flock (**I Pet. 5:1-5; Acts 20:28**)
- Ruling or guiding (**Heb. 13:17, 24; I Tim. 5:20**)
- Maturing the church (**Eph. 4:11**)
- Visiting and praying for the sick (**Jas. 5:13-18**)
- Overseeing (**I Pet. 5:1**)

These functions are not arbitrary but delegated functions. That is elders have no more rights than those, which are found in the Scriptures.

When, therefore, the term "watch" is used in relationship to elders, it carries the idea of vigilance. This idea seems to come from a study of the watchman on the tower as found in **Ezek. 3**. The function of the watchman was to look out for the enemy and give warning to the people about the impending dangers, so that they could prepare themselves. If he failed in this responsibility, then he would be held accountable for whatsoever damage was caused by the enemy. So it is with elders in the church. Elders must be on guard to protect the church from ravenous wolves and perverters of the truth and factious men. That is why the qualifications state that they are not to be recent converts but men who by a period of time, know full well the doctrine of Christ.

But not only should they watch out for attacks from without but also from within (**Acts 20:28**). Thus, they must be able to spot unspiritual characteristics in the lives of the members whose only desire is to cause confusion, dissent and other problems and try to usurp authority that is not theirs! They must watch those who are teachers for unsound teaching and preaching. They must be able to help those who display unchristian characteristics in their lives and correct them. They must also learn to use those who display good qualities and are indispensable in the ministry of the word.

Elders are not only to watch, but they are to admonish also. To admonish means to warn, to put in their minds. Notice those that they are to (**2Thess. 5:14-15**):

- Admonish the disorderly, those who are out of rank or step.
- Support the fainthearted – those who have become despondent with life and are in need of stimulation to discharge the ordinary duties of life.
- Support the weak, to help those who are strengthless.
- Be long suffering; that is to suffer long with people.

- See that none repay evil for evil, but that love is persuaded.

Elders also must feed or tend the flock among them (**I Pet. 5:2**). The idea is that of shepherding. The shepherd, Jesus said, "knows the sheep" (**Jno 10:14**). And the sheep knows the shepherd (**Jno 10:4**). The shepherd is not a hireling therefore when one goes astray he leaves the others and goes looking for the lost one. If danger approaches he defends the sheep, if need be, he gives his life for his sheep! The shepherd's staff is designed to beat with one end and to be able to reach down and gently pull the sheep out of a dangerous crevice and running water with the other. The shepherd cannot do any of these things without knowing, tending, and feeding the flock.

Shepherds do more than just lead the sheep to greener pastures. They watch, tend and comfort the sheep when they are restless, insecure, troubled, afraid, and in doubt. That's why elders cannot tend other flocks away from their local church; for too much time is needed to tend one congregation.

Elders watch, tend or feed, but they rule. The unfortunate misunderstanding of the term rule, however, has given many men a distorted and perverted concept of what the work of the elders is! This perverted concept of the word has caused the Lord's church untold damage and caused many people to lose their souls, as they become dictators and little gods in the church. The word "rule" carries with it the idea of guide. Elders are guides of God's heritage but they are not the bosses of that heritage! Some men feel that since they are elders and elders are to rule, if they can't boss they will burst, if they can't rule, they will ruin! How then are elders to rule? With an iron fist? No, a thousand times no! They are to rule through the word and, most especially, through their example of their lives as it is controlled by the word, (**Heb. 13:7**). Elders have no arbitrary power and have no more power than the evangelist!

The elders also oversee the spiritual development of the church (**Acts 20:28**)! Unfortunately, overseership has become lordship to many! To oversee to many means to sit in the rostrum and look over the assembly; or discharging a position rather than a duty.

In too many instances the only thing that elders oversee is the budget, the building, and the preacher! But Paul told them they were to oversee the flock. They were to protect and keep the flock from being infested with unsound doctrine, internal personal problems, and wolves in sheep's clothing.

Elders are to convict the gainsayer (**Tit. 1:9**). A gainsayer is one who opposes or contradicts the teaching of God's Word. Elders must be able to convince these individuals both privately and publicly. This is why the elder must not be a novice. He must be sound in the faith and have a working ability to use that word in order to keep the church pure!

Thus the job of the elder is to watch, admonish, tend or feed, and convict the gainsayer. These are areas of special spiritual men who must meet certain qualifications. You just do not hand over the job of elder to anyone!

The qualifications of elders fall into two categories:

- Positive qualifications
- Negative qualifications

In the positive qualifications, each elder, according to Paul, must all possess one of these to some degree. The word must in **I Tim.3:2** carries the idea of moral necessity or obligation. In other words, it is imperative that men who aspire to be elders to have all of these qualifications. None can be missing in one elder but found in another.

Each elder must possess all of these positive qualities:

- Temperate; self control
- Sober-minded; he must be in possession of his senses
- Orderly; he is a well-arranged, and well-ordered individual
- Hospitable, that is generous to guests
- Teacher; one who can and is able to instruct
- Gentle; fair, patient; it expresses that consideration that looks humanely and reasonable at the facts of a case

- Rules well his own house (self-explanatory)
- Children are in subjection
- Good testimony from without, a good report from non-members
- Husband of one wife, not an unmarried man, legally or otherwise
- Love of good; that which is good, decent
- Just; attempts to be fair and honest in all his judgements
- Holy different, separate
- Self-controlled; places a curb on himself
- Defender; able to uphold the truth
- Blameless; without reproach

The negative qualifications are:
- No brawler; one not given to wine or abuse
- No striker; one that is ready with a blow
- Not contentious; one who likes to dispute or quarrel
- Without reproach; open to censure
- Not self-willed; one who wishes to have his way always
- Not soon to anger; prone to anger
- Not a lover of money; a hireling

The evangelist must have a working and practical knowledge edge of work and the qualifications of men who have the desire to become elders in the church of our Lord.

As the evangelist labors with the local congregation, he must be able to instill the desire into the lives of men who can reach these lofty qualifications. He is to encourage, instruct and lead these men to achieve this divinely appointed office.

One of the ways that an evangelist help train men to be elders is by "putting his hands hastily on no man" (**I Tim. 5:22**). That is, he does not select men or give the impression that he will appoint them to the office without first knowing whether they will meet the qualifications. Herein calls for the development of interpersonal relationships and the ability to be honest and straightforward with men.

Just because a man may be faithful in attendance to all the services, he is not automatically qualified to be an elder.

A man may be faithful and dependable in coming to services, but may not have the aptitude, integrity, fortitude, stamina or wisdom to see a difficult decision through. Case in point: a woman in Oklahoma sued Elders. These men were men of great faith and tremendous courage as they stood their ground on biblical principles! These men had withdrawn from a sister who had been living in a compromising state. She in turn sued them for invasion of privacy and was awarded a judgement.

These men, however, stood their ground, challenged the court's decision – going all the way to the Supreme Court – finally being vindicated. These are the types of men that God needs. Men of integrity and fortitude.

The evangelist must know that the men he "ordains" will be men who are capable of making sound, sensible, spirit-filled decisions.

It does not take a lot of wisdom to buy building supplies but it does in dealing with the traumatic experiences that people are confronted with every day! Decisions of discipline, of indoctrination, of spiritual development, of giving sound advice to the problems of life and the ability to make God's word real in the lives of members calls for men of wisdom and spirituality. It calls for men of unique visions to see the tremendous opportunities to convert the world to Jesus, to send missionaries out and to inject and infuse congregations with worldwide evangelism.

Evangelists must be able to discern if the men who will serve as elders have this potential.

The question might be raised, where do these men come from? They come from the fruit of the work of the evangelist! When an evangelist converts a man, it is his function to instill the part of the Great Commission of "teaching to observe all things" (Matt. 28:19-20). As the evangelist instructs and the men show the willingness, the faith, the determination, the evangelist needs to implement his life into those individuals who show eldership potential. How he does it is left up to him and those men who are aspiring to the office.

Who ordains the elders? It is the function of the evangelist, according to Paul in **Titus 1:5**. Now this ordination is not an ecclesiastical function, but rather he selects the men that are qualified and presents them to the church, then based upon the church's approval, they are installed into the work. There are no prescribed plans per se as to how to ordain elders but because of the nature of the work, much prayer and fasting should be done before their selection and ordination.

The Evangelist-Elder Relationship

Of all the relationships in the local congregation, none effects the ministry like the relationship between elders and evangelists. As a matter of fact, many, if not most evangelists who resign from the work of the local church cite a "deteriorating relationship between them and the elders" or leaders as the primary cause for their resignation. Yet, where the work has been successful, generally there has been a spirit of cooperation, unity, respect, love and the willingness for the word of God to be the last standard by which all decisions are made!

The relationship between elders and the evangelist is unique in that the overall growth of the congregation is placed in their hands! Therefore, there is no room for jealousy, envy, or lack of communication. There has to be the desire that the welfare of the church must be first and foremost, and that the devil must not be allowed to play havoc with the body of Christ.

Also the evangelist must realize that elders are not his elders, but they are God's elders, and that if they have been properly trained, they ought not be passed over or selected because of his likes or dislikes of them. He should know that they are God's men first and friends and associates second.

The evangelist must also realize that God has predetermined that elders who "guide well" are to be counted worthy of "double honor" (I Tim. 5:17).

The conscientious evangelist will consider himself blessed if he has elders that the church is willing to bestow double honor on, especially if the elder is an evangelist! By the same rule, the elder must realize that if he was trained, ordained by the present evangelist, that he will not be his spiritual superior just because he has become an elder. The evangelist, by virtue of his preaching and teaching, will receive many honors from those who are grateful and appreciative of the job well done!

There should be no jockeying for position in God's kingdom. Each individual must realize that greatness comes not in the fact that one holds a specific office but by bestowing labor in God's kingdom (Matt. 20:28) and that respect and recognition comes because of their work's sake (I Thess. 5:13).

Therefore, elders and evangelists must spend time together in prayer, consultation, study and fellowship, that the lines of communication may be kept open at all times and that problems must be dealt with in a godly manner.

Because of the nature of responsibility, Satan will always try to pit elders and evangelists against each other or the church against the evangelist or elder. However, it is during these times that men of faith and spiritual integrity will humble themselves and "esteem one another better than self" (Phil. 2:3). When elders and evangelists are united, you will have a united congregation. To this end, both officers must strive. Each one must be diligent in "keeping the unity of the spirit in the bond of peace" (**Eph. 4:1-4**).

Training Deacons

The deacons of a local congregation serve a tremendous role in that they serve in capacities that keep the church moving. The term "deacon" simply means servant. The office of the deacon is vital in the work of any congregation and therefore Paul gives some serious qualifications for their election:

- Grave, serious
- Not double-tongued; not saying one thing while meaning another
- Not given too much wine; or a drunkard
- Not greedy of filthy lucre; not a hireling

- Holding the mystery of faith in good conscience; knows the truth
- Must be proven
- Blameless; not open to censure
- Husband of one wife; must be married
- Rules children well

Normally this responsibility falls on the shoulders of the evangelist and since Paul wrote Timothy to ordain, then it is therefore seen as one of the responsibilities of the evangelist.

The New Testament does not clearly define just what their total role is; therefore, deacons can serve in the following services:

- Benevolence
- Finances
- Education
- Maintenance
- And just whatever is necessary for the growth of the church

Deacons, on the other hand, must realize that they are not junior elders. Nor are they substitutes for the eldership nor are they to make decisions for the church. Deacons work under the oversight of the evangelist and elders and are responsible to the church.

Deacons must be trained so as to relieve the evangelist and elders to the care of the spiritual welfare of the church. This does not mean that the work of the deacons is not spiritual, but rather it is spiritually motivated with spiritual implications. It is more than just keeping a building clean. But rather reflects a proper attitude towards the holiness of God.

In the benevolence aspect, it shows the spiritual qualities of a God who is concerned about the physical welfare of mankind. It shows what "pure and undefiled religion" is (**Jas. 1:26-27**).

It takes unique individuals to minister to the physical needs of individuals. To the end, the evangelist must work to train men to see the tremendous service they can render to God on behalf of human redemption. It is no small matter for men to handle the business and financial affairs of the church. Therefore, the evangelist does well to take his time and see to it that men who would be deacons receive the proper training and proper motivation.

Training Teachers

The church must become a teaching factory! And one thing that the evangelist will find out is that he cannot do all the teaching! Therefore, he will need to train the faithful to be faithful teachers.

This will require the careful screening of these individuals to see if they possess the qualities of patience, love, dedication, and the desire to study and be taught to accomplish these goals. Teachers are the backbone of the church. Therefore, the evangelist will make the training of teachers one of his major priorities. He will want to establish an ongoing training program for those who would be teachers. New teachers must be recruited and trained consistently. Older teachers must be motivated and recycled. Teachers must be trained to recognize potential problem areas and help the leadership to address them.

Teachers must also be trained in techniques and diverse usage of materials. They must be trained to have the ability to teach diverse materials as well as becoming specialists in given areas of teaching.

The smart evangelist will make this his special interest since it is this area that will keep the church healthy. He should work to train an individual to be the educational director. He then must be trained to select department heads and teachers. He must learn how to interpret the needs of the church, and how to devise curriculums to meet those needs.

One of the ways to utilize time and energy is to find someone within the school system preferably administration, who has that "know how" already and who possess the qualities of humility, faith, and love for the Lord. The training will then be mostly centered on the Word of God.

Teachers must be trained to recognize that there is more to teaching than just standing before a class and delivering a lecture. In order to be most effective, communication with students is essential; and personal involvement will be more than just showing up on Sunday or during the mid-week for a performance! They need to be made aware that they are to be caretakers of those students placed in their class or their oversight. Therefore, there will be phone calls to make and cards to be sent. Sometimes it will involve the discipline of an unruly student, while at other times the student may need their time. Teachers must also learn that they are barometers of potential problems in the church. The deceiver can introduce false concepts; therefore they must be on the lookout for the infusion of false ideas into the classroom.

Teachers must be made aware of the difficulties of teaching, the eternal consequences (**Jas. 3:1**), and much of the frustration that comes along with the teaching profession.

There are many dangers that confront the teacher. The wise evangelist will work to create an atmosphere where many potential dangers are checked before they spread. A program that provides challenges and incentives, and which shows appreciation for the efforts of the teachers can eliminate stress, burnout, cynicism and lost enthusiasm. Teacher's banquets appreciation dinners and special awards can help maintain teachers who are the backbone of any congregation. Also a pulpit that will encourage and exhort the fine work of the teachers serves as a good motivation for the continual development of teachers.

Training the Church

Aged men

Another area of training often overlooked by many evangelists is the fact that besides training of other evangelists, elders, deacons, and teachers, he is also commanded to train "aged men" to be:

- Temperate; that is to be self-controlled
- Grave; that is serious
- Sober-minded; in other words, the mind is sound
- Sound in faith; to have a healthy faith
- Sound in love; a healthy active goodwill towards all others
- Sound in patience; to be steadfast in his commitments to the Lord (**Titus 2:1-2**)

He is also to train the "aged women" that they be:

- Reverent in demeanor; the behavior should be fitting of sacred character
- Not slanderous; or a false accuser and spreader of innuendoes and false criticisms of the church
- Not a slave of wine; one who is dependent on wine

- Teachers; not necessarily in the classroom sense, but in the one on one approach

Who and what should they teach?

- Teach that which is good
- Train younger women to:
  - ○ Love their husbands
  - ○ Love their children
  - ○ To be sober minded; having a sound mind
  - ○ Be chaste; that is pure from carnal desires
  - ○ Be workers at home; homemakers
  - ○ Be kind, good; to be beneficent in their effect
  - ○ Be in subjection
  - ○ So that God's word is not blasphemed (**Tit. 2:3-6**).
  - ○ The evangelist is to train young men to be sound in their minds (**Tit. 2:7**).

In today's world of protest and protesters, the evangelist must train the members of the church to be in subjection to the civil authorities. In an age of disobedience and lack of respect for authority, the evangelist must train the church to respect the law of the land, and to obey not just the letter, but be ready to assist in any worthwhile endeavor. Christians must realize that God has given the civil authority to men, and

Christians must respect it as long as it does not conflict with God's Word!

SECTION THREE

Setting in Order

One of the difficult works of the evangelist generally occurs when he takes over a work that has gone down. In **Titus 1:5**, Paul gave Titus a commission: Not to necessarily add to what the apostle himself had done, but that he was to set things right again which had fallen into disorder since the apostle had labored at Crete. This setting in order calls for re-teaching, retraining, and reestablishment of things once done by a local congregation as taught by the word of God.

There are many things that can get out of order in a church, which does not have a capable evangelist. Once this happens it becomes the function of the evangelist to set those things back in order.

- Worship
- Evangelism and missions

- Benevolence
- Discipline
- Governmental structure

In the building up of a new work, these things will take care of themselves as the evangelist administers his duties. It is in the setting in order of things that the evangelist needs administrative capabilities, motivational skills and "dogged-determination" to carry out his work.

The Worship of the New Testament Church

The worship of the New Testament church is a unique and simple act. Yet, it has the most tremendous effects on the worshippers in that it can lead one to glory or to damnation!

Worship is an act of homage, a rendering of obeisance, an acknowledgment of something greater than man is himself. He who tells him how to worship has restricted the worship of the New Testament church!

How to Worship

The worship of the New Testament church is limited to two elements (**Jno. 4:24**):

- Spirit
- Truth

Outside of these two aspects all other forms of worship are to be disregarded and rejected.

When we speak of spirit, we are speaking about the right attitude, atmosphere, reverence and disposition. When we speak of truth, we are speaking of that which is revealed by the word. Remember, Jesus said, "Thy word is truth" (**Jno. 17:17**). Since God has limited himself to accept only those two elements of worship, the evangelist must put into order the worship of God based upon these two elements. Anything, therefore, not authorized by the word as Spirit and Truth cannot be in order!

This, therefore, calls for the evangelist to know what the worship of the New Testament was like in the first century. The Bible tells us but so does history. In a world full of misconception and false teachings, sometimes history has an enormous influence in understanding the Word of God. We recognize that the Bible is still our guide and that history just corroborates God's truth.

History tells us, according to Justin Martyr:

But we, after we have thus washed him who has been convinced and has assented to Our teaching, bring him to the place where those who are called brethren, are assembled, in order that we may offer hearty prayers in common for ourselves and for the baptized person, and for all others in every place, that we may be counted worthy, now also be found good citizens and keepers of the commandments, so that we may be saved with an everlasting salvation. Having ended the prayer we salute one with a holy kiss.

There is then brought to the president of the brethren, bread and a cup of wine mixed with water; and he taking them, gives praise and glory to the father of the universe, through the name of the Son and of the Holy Ghost, and offer thanks at a considerable length for our being counted worthy to receive these things at his hands. And when he has concluded the prayers and thanksgiving, all the people present express their assent by saying **amen**. The word "Amen" answers in the Hebrew language to genoits (so let it be). And when the president has given thanks and all the people have expressed their assent, those who are called by us deacons give to each of those present to partake of the bread and wine mixed with water over the thanksgiving was pronounced, and to those who are absent they carry away a portion.

And the food is called among us (**Eucharist**) the Eucharist of which no one is allowed to partake but the man who believes that the things, which we teach, are true, and who has been washed with the washing that if for the remission of sins, and regeneration, and who is so living as Christ has enjoined. And we afterwards continually are reminding each other of these things. And the wealthy among us help the needy; and we always keep together. And for all things wherewith we are supplied we bless the making of all through his Son, Jesus Christ, and through the Holy Ghost. And on the day called Sunday, all who live in cities or in the country gather together to one place, and the memories of the apostles or the writings of the prophets are read, as long as time permits; then, when the reader has ceased, the president verbally instructs and exhorts to the emulation of these good things. Then we all rise together and pray; and as we before said, when our prayers is ended bread, wine and water are brought and the president in like manner offers prayers and thanksgiving, according to his ability, and the people assent, saying "Amen" and then there is distribution to each, and a participation of that over which thanks has been given, and to those who are absent a portion is sent by the deacons. And they who are well to do and willing, give what each thinks fit; and what is collected is deposited with the president, who succors the orphans and widows and those who through sickness or any other cause are in want, and those who are in bonds, and the sojourners among us, and in a word take care of all who are in need. But Sunday is the day on which we hold our common assembly, because it is the first day on which God having wrought a change in the darkness and matter, made the world, and Jesus Christ our Savior on the same day rose from the dead, for He was crucified on the day before that of Saturn, (Saturday). And on the day after that of Saturn, which is the day of the sun, having appeared to his apostles and disciples, He taught them these things, which we must have submitted to you also for your consideration. (Justin Martyr, "Apology" Chps. 65-67, Ante-Nicene Fathers, Vol. 1 pp.185-186)

Although this is a long quotation, we see that at the end of the century the church still had a simple form of worship consisting of prayer, communion, exhortation, giving and praying.

The evangelist must see to it that this be set in order. Not a routine of 1-2-3-4-5, but that each item of worship be according to the truth, reverent and be conducted in such a manner that God receives the glory!

Too many of our worship services today are a show of emotional outbursts or are deader than a corpse! The evangelist must see to it that the church understands that our services should be characterized by life because our God is alive. Gimmickry or sensationalism should not be employed.

Someone has said that we have tried everything to liven up our services from tea parties, ice cream suppers and chicken dinners. Subsequently, we (the church) have become as cold as ice cream, dead as chicken and weak as tea. This should not be. We serve a God who wants us to serve Him by authority and faith in what He has directed. Therefore, in setting in order things that are lacking, the evangelist must use the Word of God as his authority.

Singing

In the service, the singing should be accapella that is without the use or accompaniment of mechanical instruments of music. This was characteristic of the first century church because it was ordained of God. The evangelist should teach the church how the church of the first century, living in the shadows of the apostles, had followed their instructions by singing as they (the apostles) had specified. Such passages as **Ephesians 5:19, Colossians 3:16 and I Corinthians 14:15** need to be explained and reinforced in their context to show that the first century church did not use mechanical instruments of music.

Music is a generic term, but God specified the type of music he wanted. There are two types of music:

- Instrumental
- Accapella

He (God) chose accapella music. For some six hundred years there were no instruments of music in usage in the services of the church. Only vocal music was used. This should tell us something.

In teaching the church about singing the evangelist can show the church how the Bible teaches us:

- Direct command
- Approved example
- Necessary inference

Singing is a direct and specific command. Therefore, all other forms are excluded! Absolutely no one should be a spectator in the worship assembly of God. All must be personally involved, and this is one way to do it!

Prayer

In the service of the Lord, the prayer should be led by men whose lives are reflective of honesty, sincerity and holiness (**I Tim. 2:8**).

Prayer should be made in the form of supplication, intercession, and thanksgiving for all men, especially for those who are in high places! This is to be done so that the Christian community can lead a tranquil and quiet life (**I Tim. 2:1-3**).

The prayer life of the church must occupy a place of importance in the order of service. It should not be run through or rushed! Enough time should be allotted and no one should be baited with the words, "Brother 'So and So' will lead us in a short word of prayer."

The church should show its respect and reverence to God by assuming a spirit of humility, contrition and awe! For prayer takes place in the throne room of heaven, therefore, it should not be uttered while members are walking around, talking or unprepared to approach the throne of God.

The evangelist can take the lead by being a man of much prayer and with much fervency.

Prayer should be specific as well as generic and must be directed to the God of the universe. It should be accompanied by faith, hope, and love. It should not be mere vain talking, but should be an outpouring from the heart. It should receive affirmation from the congregation.

Prayer must receive the proper order in order for it to be effective and beneficial to the church. "Without prayer the church becomes weak," therefore, much instruction and preparation needs to go into making the public prayer a dynamic time for the church. It is the function of the evangelist to teach men to pray in such a way that they can lead us to the very throne of God and into His divine presence.

The evangelist must realize that the church can be hindered by men who are bereft of spiritual awareness, whose prayers are mere words, empty of power, vague in meaning, sounding good but without any real impact. Prayer is the lifeblood of the congregation and in the assembly of the church, it should be done to the glory and honor of God the Father!

Communion

In setting things in order, the evangelist must be aware of becoming stoic and ritualistic in the observance of the Lord's Supper. Our gathering is for the purpose of proclaiming the death of Christ and for the celebration of His resurrection! Here, as in the before mentioned acts of worship, the evangelist must see to it that the true meaning of communion is not lost as we hasten through the services.

The Lord's Supper is, first of all, a commandment (**I Cor. 11:24**). Secondly, it is a cross examination of one's self (**I Cor. 11:27-29**). The communion is consolatory (**I Cor. 11:26**), and the evangelist must see to it that those who lead know these things and convey them to the church.

The communion is a commemoration and, therefore, the service must reflect that in its observation. It should be done reverently, discreetly, and with the utmost respect. Every member should be encouraged to be on time and to remember the ongoing sacrifice that was made by Jesus on behalf of all mankinds.

Men who understand the unique significance of this event

should lead the communion. Special care should be given to the carrying out of it and he who leads should encourage each member's participation.

A series of lessons might be presented on the uniqueness and place of the communion in the worship services. Its elements, its purpose, its benefits and privileges that are accorded the child of God in its participation, should help the church to understand what a great privilege God has blessed man with! It is essential that the general membership understands the spiritual implications of this event, and that they understand fully the results of improper attitudes towards the communion!

These lessons should be incorporated into the preaching program of the church as well as the ongoing part of indoctrination of new converts.

Giving

The evangelist must realize that the Bible has much to say about finances. If there is one area that a Christian should not be defunct in, it is this area of giving.

Giving is a grace bestowed by God on his children. Every Christian should consider his giving with the light of 2 Corinthians chapters 8 through 9.

The evangelist must keep before the people what giving is all about. It is a commandment from God according to Paul in **I Cor. 16:1-2**. It is a grace, and to be a great giver is to exemplify that God is appreciated in our lives.

Giving must be according to purpose. A purpose is an intention, an aim or an objective. Therefore, the church must be taught to give systematically rather than in a haphazard manner, (**I Cor. 16:1-2; 2 Cor. 9:7; 8:12**). Giving should be done with liberality in mind (**Mt. 5:20, I Cor. 8:1-3, 14**). Christians should be of Solomon's counsel in **Prov. 11:25**, "The liberal soul shall be made fat." Giving should be a joyous occasion, not a burdensome and cumbersome feeling or affair (**2 Cor. 8:3-5; 9:7**).

Giving shows the depth of one's love, the debt of gratitude one has for God and His cause.

The evangelist must instill this in the church. A lack of adequate giving says that the church is out of order!

The evangelist must see to it that members are kept informed as to the status of the financial affairs of the church, as well as all other aspects.

In the collection of the saints, Christians should be encouraged and not browbeaten into giving that which should be a gift based on love and thanksgiving. It would be very useful to present a series of lessons on giving once a year and to set up a Bible class on this important subject once a year.

The Act of Preaching

This should be the evangelist's hour. He should have spent

time with the Word of God and now he should have something from God's word upon which to speak. He should not use the pulpit to expound philosophical arguments or preconceived ideas. But rather his preaching should be with the idea of meeting some particular need of that membership. This would require knowledge of the members and their needs.

It will require much time in study and prayer, plus adequate preparations. Members should be encouraged to avail themselves of every opportunity to hear God's word preached! In so doing the evangelist will turn the church into a teaching factory where the primary aim is to learn God's word, implement it into one's life and, then, pass on that which has been learned!

To this end, the evangelist must be a person who is prepared to speak in such a way that the youngest to the oldest will be able to understand.

Much preaching that is being done today is a deductive type of preaching. This type of preaching presents a conclusion at the start, and then it gives the reasons and facts for its conclusion. This type of preaching makes Christians spectators and leaves them somewhat empty. This type of preaching tends to teach doctrines, but very seldom deals with the actual needs of the church. Lives are not changed! Christ-likeness is not seen. Phariseeism tends to develop, and in the words of one writer, "Christians become hardheaded!"

What type of preaching should the evangelist do? He should do the same type of preaching that Jesus did. The type he showed his disciples and the type found both within the Old and New Testaments. Jesus took men where they were, addressed their situations, made applications and then allowed those who heard to make up their own minds about what he taught. This type of preaching caused prostitutes to repent, tax collectors to renounce their thievery, and Pharisees to turn and follow Jesus. It caused burly fishermen to weep, soldiers to admit, "Never a man so spake", and the populace to say, "We never heard it in that fashion!"

The evangelist that uses the word of God, the circumstances of life and makes the proper applications will see a changed church. He will see lives that are renewed, spirits that are rekindled, talents that glorify God, souls won to Christ, sin repudiated, and a church that is alive and vibrant!

Remember that the "poor heard him gladly" but the religious did not want to hear him. It was the religious who knew all the answers, who had all the right arguments, and who were the elite that put him on the cross!

Evangelism and Missions

Once a church is set in order in the realm of edification, it should then cast its eyes to the shores of lost humanity. This does not mean that no evangelism is ongoing in the process of setting in order, for evangelism is certainly going on in the preaching and teaching of God's word. But we are speaking of the fact that things must be done decently and in order before a major thrust into the realm of humanity should take place.

The evangelist must, here, be an example of the mission of the church as it relates to propagating the message of salvation to lost mankind.

It is the function of the body of Christ to spread the message of Christ (**Mt. 28:18-20**) to every creature on the face of the earth (**Mk. 16:16-20**).

However, the carrying out of the great commission calls for careful planning, training and implementation. Every congregation has the solemn responsibility to "go into all the world and preach the Gospel to every creature", but you don't want to duplicate efforts. Therefore one sees the necessity for proper planning and implementation.

Every evangelist must see to it that every member is exposed to the great commission as he carries it out in view of the church. He should establish training opportunities for learning how to be evangelistic and how to share the good news, whether he does it by training each individual in a one-on-one relationship, or through the classroom or pulpit.

He must teach it, preach it, and live it. His sermons should reverberate with the context of the great commission. He must encourage, motivate and lead in this field. He should praise those who have "tasted the blood" of seeing someone else come to the Lord. Those who are constantly striving to bring others out of the bondage of sin must also be continually motivated and encouraged.

The wise evangelist will strive for long-term evangelism. That is he will train with the future in mind, rather than for the immediate presence alone. This calls for long-range goals as well as short-range goals, along with the planning and implementation. The wise evangelist will always be training faithful youngsters to be evangelistically inclined and committed to the cause of Christ. This is one way to insure the church of future evangelists, and to make sure that the teachings of the New Testament church is preserved.

One of the great needs of the Lord's church is the foreign mission which holds about only ten percent of the world population. This means that ninety percent of the gospel preachers are concentrating on only ten percent of the world population! How then can the church fulfill its worldwide responsibility of evangelizing the world? Herein is where the evangelist must point the church to worldwide evangelism, and challenge it to take the gospel to every creature.

The evangelist must, here, make plans so that the church can be in a position to support a work and, at the same time, prepare the church to not only support an evangelist in the mission field financially but also to go and do evangelism work on the mission field. This would be one way for a congregation to feel the responsibility and see the need of the worldwide commission. Members of a congregation would be more inclined to fully support a foreign mission work if they saw the need first hand.

As the population of the world increases, the necessity for missionaries becomes more imperative. Also, because of the economic situation, many evangelists in America may have to go to work and support themselves in the preaching of God's word in order for local congregations to carry out the mission of evangelism.

The local evangelist must not neglect local missionary efforts as well. There are many areas here where the church is not known. Even in what is known as the Bible belt, there are thousands of counties that do not have any congregations of the Lord's people. The evangelist must mobilize the church to reach out to these communities. Plans should be made to select one of these areas and plans should be made as how to effectively evangelize that local community. Perhaps a religious survey could be taken then an analysis of the survey. A site might be selected either to host a gospel meeting or to conduct some type of door knocking campaign with the purpose of getting into the homes of individuals and teaching them. Also, a team might be trained to evangelize and to move into the community and put down roots in the community for the purpose of one-on-one evangelism. The point of this is that every evangelist should be willing to do this.

Every effort should be made for congregational support, financially, morally and emotionally. Also, much prayer should be made by the membership for the success of the work.

Much care should be given in the establishment of a new congregation. Just because a congregation sponsors a work does not mean that it is in control of that work. Each local congregation is autonomous; that is self-ruled. The sponsoring congregation must allow the work to develop its own leadership, its own financial responsibility, and to eventually become self-supporting. The sponsoring congregation should work with this in mind. It should not allow the new work to become a parasite nor to remain dependent on the sponsoring church any longer than necessary. It should be weaned, as it is able to take care of itself.

Thus, the work of the evangelist takes the lead in seeing to it that this important area of work is carried out. This takes long-range planning and much effort therefore much prayer is needed. It will take the proper motivation and the proper amount of financial resources to insure adequate support. One way to insure the proper finance is to set aside a certain amount of the weekly budget. One can begin by putting aside one percent of the budget and add on a percentage at a five-percentage amount until the church is putting fifty percent of its budget into missions. This is the work of the Lord's church and it should be given the utmost attention, care and stimulation. The church is in existence to make known the manifold grace of God to a lost and perishing world.

The Local Church and Benevolence

The Lord's work always seems to be interwoven with more than just some single act. The church is its own benevolent society. The church has a responsibility to be a charitable organization. Members must be taught that they are their own brother's keepers. That they are to "do good to all men, especially those of the household of faith." (**Gal. 6:10**) James wrote that "pure and undefiled religion was to visit the fatherless and the widows in their affliction and to keep one's self unspotted from the world." (**Jas. 1:26-27**).

One of the great witnesses that the early church gave to the world was its witness of benevolence. Let the record speak: "They sold their possessions, they had all things common, no one lacked for anything, distribution was made to those who were in need." (**Acts 2:44; 5:1-10**)

James and John tie benevolence to one's claim of being God's child. (**Jas. 2:15, I John 3:16**)

The evangelist must train the church to be responsive to the needs of its members and those of the world. To this end, the evangelist must organize and mobilize the church to have such things that are necessary to carry out this ministry. This can be done in several ways. A committee may be set up with the deacons in charge and some faithful brother along with the faithful sisters who will be responsible in giving to those in needs. Also, individuals who may be able to offer specific types of help can be enlisted and be used in certain spots. The benevolent church does more than give out canned goods and clothing, they provide furniture, places to stay, money in emergency situations, someone to baby-sit, or help clean up, providing modes of transportation, counseling, helping people set up budgets and sitting with the infirmed.

Some of these areas call for professional help and most congregations have people with professional experience who are not involved in the work of the church and would gladly help if called upon. The purpose of benevolence:

- To help the person to be relieved of his particular problem or misfortune.
- To establish a relationship with Jesus Christ
- To glorify God
- That the world may see God at work in the life of a Christian

Any church with a strong benevolence program will have a good evangelistic program. For many that are in need of physical help will generally listen to those who help them fulfill their needs. Any congregation with a good evangelistic program will have to have a good benevolent program for it will, in its thrust to win souls, find people who are destitute and in need.

Setting in Order the Governmental Structure of the Church

When Paul told Titus in **Titus 1:5** to "set in order the things that are wanting." He told him also, to "ordain elders in every city." This charge qualified the young evangelist to see about the administration of the church.

Of all the work an evangelist does in a local congregation, no one aspect of that work will have as much impact as the ordination of elders in that congregation. This is a most serious matter and should not be taken lightly! Paul warned Timothy, 'to lay hands hastily on no man" **(I Tim. 5:22)** when it came to selecting elders for the church.

How does the evangelist ordain elders? Does he arbitrarily and indiscriminately select them? Does he use a committee to screen and certify them? To be honest, this verse gives the evangelist only the right to recommend to the church, men whom he knows meet the qualifications for the office. He is not at liberty to select men to serve as elders without the consent of the church.

The evangelist must know these men better than the church. He must know that the qualifications ordained by the Holy Spirit are met to some degree in their lives. He must know their motives for desiring the office and, at the same time, whether they will be men of unquestionable faith! This, therefore, calls for an intimate relationship. He will have to spend time in the training of these men, in their home, in social surroundings, when they are wrestling with different types of decisions. He will have to see them under fire as well as in times of smooth sailing.

Before they have become elders they ought to have been tested! If deacons must "be first proven" (**I Tim. 3:10**), what about those men whose work it will be to give God an answer for the condition that his church is in? Someone may say, "How do you test elders?" Make them deacons! If they refuse to do the work of deacons, what makes you think they will be humble enough to serve as elders?

In selecting men to be presented to the church, the evangelist should be aware of the culture, environment, and social atmosphere a man comes from. Not every Christian who comes from a poor environment will be 'poor in spirit.' As a matter of fact, he may see the office of the eldership not as a work, but as a way to "lord" over people, particularly the evangelist. Not just because a man is successful does it mean that he is rich in faith. The evangelist must be aware of the ego of men! He must, to the best of his ability, see to it that these men selected are God-fearing individuals, whose motives are pure and whose objectives are to further the cause of Christ!

Once the qualifications of each individual are ascertained by the evangelist he then presents them to the church, giving the church sufficient time to bring forth any accusations which are Scripturally right; not personality conflicts, but legitimate, spiritual accusations. If none is forthcoming, and then a day should be appointed in which these men will receive their public charge and installed. This must be a joyous occasion, yet the most serious. Therefore, prayer and fasting should accompany this process.

Once elders are ordained, the congregation must realize that elders are no the superior of the evangelist. It is precisely here that the evangelist and elders must have a strong working relationship, for there are many weak people in the body, who because of likes and dislikes, will pit the evangelist against the elders and vice versa. If the relationship is not right the church will suffer. The work of the evangelist is to set in order the church and ordain elders. Therefore, he has been given God's authority to do so. He does not relinquish this authority because elders have been ordained! Elders die, disqualify themselves, move, get old and lose interest. Therefore, the training and development of men to serve as elders is an ongoing process.

Elders must concern themselves with the caring of that flock, its spiritual needs as well as its emotional and physical needs. They should not feel threatened by an evangelist who is doing his work. Elders have an area of responsibility, and so does the evangelist. And when either one get out of line, it is the responsibility of one to keep the others on goal. The disciplining of each other is vital if the work is to succeed! The evangelist is to accept accusations against the elders only at the mouth of "two or three witnesses." (**I Tim. 5:19**) Those that sin are to be "rebuked publicly". In this area the work of the evangelist should be in love and honor with restoration in view, never vindictive or punitive.

The evangelist must also realize that he is to "submit himself unto the elders." (**Eph. 5:21**) when he has strayed from the right path. He should accept their rebuke, correction, and admonishment without fear or resentment.

Often times the question is raised about churches who have no elders? In this instance, the evangelist as he works with faithful men, can use them in positions that are essential for the further development of the church. If in the future, men qualify themselves, then the evangelist must appoint them to the eldership.

There is also a popular notion that a church can be Scripturally unorganized! By this is meant that the church can be Scriptural, but is unorganized because it has no elders! No church is unorganized if it is scriptural! The church is not composed of just elders and deacons. The church is composed of baptized believers! Elders show a church that is maturing and growing. And the fact that a church has no elders is not a sign of unscriptuality.

No evangelist should be in a rush to ordain men to keep positions in the church without truly having a first hand knowledge of them. Much prayer and training should go into this facet of the evangelist's work! The evangelist must realize that haste makes waste. Paul encourages Timothy to "lay hands suddenly on no man." **(I Tim. 5:22)** Since the Bible, in reality, does not give us a set pattern for the ordination of elders, each congregation will have to determine how best to go about the process of selecting these men whose function are to be spiritual leaders. Whatever method a congregation selects it should not contradict any known passage of Scripture. When this is assured, whatever will work for that local church must and should be respected!

Defending the Faith

'Hold fast the form of sound words, which thou has heard of me, in faith and love which is Jesus Christ. that good thing which was committed unto these keep by the Holy Ghost which dwelleth in us." **(2 Tim. 1:13-14)**

Of all the duties of the evangelist, none is more challenging and taxing than that of defending the faith! Herein lies the true gift of the evangelist! Why? Because in defending the truth, he first of all, "must know the truth." And often time he will find as he studies that he does not truly know the truth but that he is a by-product of false indoctrination, custom and tradition, unproven assumptions, or the clone of some evangelist or school or preaching.

In order for the evangelist to defend the faith, he must be an honest, sincere, and unbiased individual in his quest for the truth! If he has preconceived ideas about everything, they would naturally disqualify him as an honest and diligent student of the word.

To this end, the evangelist must have unswerving faith that Bible is God's sole source of revelation and guidance for mankind in this present day and age. And that it must be defended to the best of one's ability with dogged determination against all those who would pervert its message without alienating the truth seeker as he stops the mouths of false, misinformed and erring teachers.

Here the evangelist must not "strive, but be gentle towards all, apt to teach, forbearing in meekness, correcting them that oppose themselves. If peradventure God may give them repentance unto the knowledge of the truth and they may recover themselves out of the snare of the devil, or having been taken captive by him unto his will." **(2 Tim. 2:24)**

In other words, before the evangelist can defend the faith, his attitude, his faith must be what God has ordained of those he seeks to correct! How then does the evangelist defend the faith?

Paul's charge to Timothy was to "hold fast." The words "hold fast" mean steadfast adherence to the faith. This holding fast was to be done to the "form" of sound words. The word "form" is from the word, "hupotiposis," which means an outline, sketch. This word comes from the Greek word "tupos," which means pattern or mold. This pattern is both recognizable and reproducible therefore it is defensible. We do no know what "form" was but whatever it was, Timothy was to have steadfast adherence to it.

It is obvious that the church at Ephesus was being bombarded with some type of false teaching. The early church had two major camps to contend with, both from within and from without. These two camps were the Judaizers and Gnostics. They had to be defeated in order for the proclamation of the

Gospel to have the results God intended for it to have.

Paul instructs the evangelist to hold fast the word against these heresies.

In **I Timothy 1:3**, Paul cites the reason for leaving Timothy at Ephesus. That he "might charge certain men not to teach a different doctrine." This doctrine, from the context, seems to have been the Judaistic concept of binding the precept of circumcision and adhering to the ordinances of the old Mosaic Law as a prerequisite for being a faithful Christian.

This caused tremendous problems to the new converts, since most of them were not of the Jewish background. Therefore, because of this false teaching the Judaizers made "shipwreck" of the faith of many of these converts (**I Tim. 1:19-20**). They had "overthrown the faith" of others (**2 Tim. 2:18**). They had in essence turned to "vain janglings." (**I Tim. 1:6**) In other words what they were teaching was empty, without any good sense. It was speculative doctrine based upon "fables and genealogies."

The other problem that the church had to contend with was that of the philosophy of Gnosticism. This philosophy, if left unchecked, would have crippled the claims of the Gospel in that it made light of the nature of Jesus Christ.

The claim of the Gnostics was basically one that dethroned God. It maintained that Spirit was good and matter was evil. Therefore, the God of the Old Testament could not have been the true God since the creation was matter, and matter was evil. It was therefore their contention that in order to arrive at the steps of the true God; one needed to come to them for special light, insight and key words that would unlock the key mystery of God.

Based on their supposition, the God of the Old Testament was one of a series of emanations emitting from the one true spiritual God until the God of the Old Testament got so far away that he could deal with matter which was considered evil.

In order to reconcile the redemptive claims of Christ, they repudiated the concept of a bodily resurrection; as a matter of fact they denounced the concept of the incarnation. They sought to make Jesus a spiritual resurrected phantom.

These erroneous concepts led to too great dangers: 1) Asceticism's and 2) Licentiousness. These two concepts would certainly destroy the basis of Christianity and its resulting freedom.

Because the Gnostics believed that body was evil, then a person could only do one of two things: He could deny its every urge, need and desire, or it could just let the body do whatsoever it wanted. Nothing would happen to the spirit of man and therefore it would be saved.

This perversion would have wrecked the church. But under the spirit's control and leadership, Paul and John wrote treatise in defense of the fact that man is accountable to God for his actions. They reasoned and showed that Jesus is indeed the true God in the incarnate state. That he literally resurrected from the grave and that he was no spiritual phantom. The books of **John, Colossians**, portions of **I Timothy** and the epistles of **John** were written to diffuse this philosophy. A complete discussion and its subsequent results can be found in William Barclays' commentary *The All-Sufficient Christ!*

These problems were met by the evangelists of the first century. There were many other problems besides these major areas of doctrine: problems of "grace and law," "division," "circumcision," "the place of the dead," "Heaven and Hell," "marriage," "gifts," "money" and every theological problem had to be handled.

Not all problems came because of internal theological conflicts. There was also the misconception of what Christians were their refusal to hail Caesar or compromise their convictions. They were seen as a threat to the Roman Empire claim of Emperor worship and a threat to all the other state religions. Then the persecution that arose while Nero was Emperor and later with the ascension of Domition to the throne.

Today's Evangelist must be on guard for modern Judaizers who bind things on the body of Christ, which cannot be sustained from the scriptures. Nor must he be surprised at the diverse and often complexities of problems that are confronting modern society, as well as those of his flock.

Today's Evangelist must of necessity have counseling skills if he is to meet the ever perplexing and changing emotional web of problems that taxes this generation. Emotional problems are an ever-increasing part of today's ministries. Therefore, the Evangelist must be proficiently trained in these areas.

The Discipline of the Church

When one considers the church and its function as well as its purpose in the world, it must have discipline! Discipline, as defined means, "mental or moral training, rules for regulating conduct, control, or order by enforcing obedience." It also means to 'train, control or punish."

Biblically speaking, it means, "the saving of the mind, admonishing, or calling to soundness of mind."

As the evangelist carries out his ministry many unruly and gainsaying disciples of the devil will enter the flock. The evangelist must ever be on watch for sin and its influence in the congregation. God has mandated in His word that the church be disciplined. Now there are two types of discipline. There is, first of all, preventive discipline, which is administered through training, teaching and admonishing. This type of discipline is done in order to prevent the second form of discipline. This form of discipline is punitive discipline. This is the administration of corrective procedures after the violation of preventive measures have been taken."

Methods of Discipline

As to the methods of discipline found in the Bible, there are three forms

- Over discipline **(Eph. 6:1-3)**. This is where the punishment for the violation far exceeds the offense.
- Under discipline. This is the administration of weak measures in implementation of both preventive and punitive discipline **(I Cor. 5:1-8)**.
- On-time discipline **(Gal. 2:4-5)**. This is the discipline that is both instructive and corrective. Its implementation is both feasible and reasonable and its corrective measure befits the transgression and is done as needed.

Results of Discipline

When discipline is carried out, three things will happen:
- There will be a maturing process **(1 Cor 5:2)**
- Obedience will be enforced **(2 Cor. 2.9)**
- Correction and purging will take place **(I Cor. 5:5)**

Who Needs Discipline?

The Bible also points out those who need discipline:

- Those who "walk disorderly" (**2 Thess. 3:6; I Thess. 5:12**). The "Disorderly" means those who are out of step. They are not walking according to God's word. This particular situation has arisen out of a misunderstanding of Paul's letter concerning the Second Coming of Christ. Some of the Christians apparently had quit working and had become parasites on the church.

- "Sexual Perverts" (**I Cor. 5:9-11**). Paul classifies these as fornicators, which is the illicit practices of unmarried individuals, whether they are effeminate; those whose characteristics are soft and feminine or the homosexual; those who prefer sex with those of the same sex. Also, those who have sex with animals.

- "Subversives and those who are contrary" to sound doctrine (**Rom. 16:17-18**)

- "Contentious" (**Tit. 3:10-11**). Those who are quarrelsome and always argumentative.

- "Doctrine Perverts" (**Phil. 3:21; Gal. 2:5; Tit. 1:0**). Those who would corrupt the word of God and transgress by teaching false doctrine and opposing the truth.

How to Administer Discipline

The question arises, how does the evangelist administer discipline to those areas. He does it:

- Through training (**2 Tim. 2:2**)
- Through admonishing or warning (**I Thess 5:14; Tit. 3:1-10**)
- Through marking or identifying and by keeping an attentive observation on anyone that is suspicious (**Rom 16:17-18**)
- Through public withdrawal or shrinking back (**2 Thess. 3:6**)
- Through shunning or avoiding (**Tit 3:10**)
- By having no fellowship with them, socially or spiritually (**I Cor. 5:9-11**)
- By turning them over to the Devil (**I Cor 5:5**)

In order to fulfill this divine mandate regarding discipline, the evangelist must train the church as to its responsibility of restoring the erring (**Gal. 6:1-2**). If this reconciliation fails, then they must realize their responsibility to support such actions in order that the person's soul might be saved from condemnation.

This responsibility should take place in visiting and encouraging them to repent and return to the church (**Mt. 18:15**). They should be the ones who carry out the action of sanctioning the withdrawal (**I Cor. 5:1-5**).

The evangelist must also see to it that members understand their attitudes and disposition. The church should know that this is a time of "mourning and deep sorrow" (**I Cor. 5:2**), looking at themselves lest they be tempted (**Gal. 6:1-2**). And once the action takes place they should not become embittered against those who have been disciplined, but should view them as those who are erring brothers who are in need of repentance and restitution (**2 Thess. 3:15**).

The Purpose of Discipline

Because there may be the tendency to publicly chastise someone who disagrees with the evangelist, he must remember the purpose for which God has ordained discipline.

- "To save the soul" (**I Cor. 5:5**). This is the ultimate goal and objective for church discipline.
- "Keep the church pure" (**I Cor. 5:6**). In order for the church to accomplish her mission in the world, she must reflect the character of Him who she serves. (**I Pet. 1:6**).
- "Keep the doctrine sound" (**Rom. 16:17-18**). The term doctrine means teaching. The wrong teaching will damn a person's soul to Hell. Therefore, the need to keep the truth pure is a vital necessity.

- "Please God" (**I Tim. 2:4**). In keeping God's word we will be pleasing to God, provided our motives and attitudes are right.
- "Be a light to the world." (**I Cor. 6:1-20**)
- To "shame the offender." (**2 Thess. 3:14**)
- To "reconcile the offender and the offended. (**Mt. 18:15**)

If discipline is not for the purpose of strengthening or purging the church, then it is of no use. God holds the evangelist responsible for setting the motion of the disciplinary process. If he does not implement it then the church will suffer untold damage. No church can exist in a society where there is no discipline. The Corinthian church is the classic example of an undisciplined church. It had every conceivable problem there was, from division to denial of the resurrection. Here was a church that needed a double dosage of God's word. Because of their lack of discipline they brought shame to the name, character and purpose of God's activity.

The evangelist must so teach that every facet of discipline is covered and implemented. Every member must be so trained that he responds in love and kindness and without hesitation to every act of biblical discipline that is implemented.

Excommunication withdrawal of fellowship is a most traumatic experience: Of all the functions of the evangelist, none can be more traumatic as having to withdraw fellowship from someone that he loves and cares for. Even though his motive and purpose may be to please God, the evangelist will invariably run into problem, misunderstandings and open hostility as he tries to install discipline in the church. Many times his motives will be questioned and his character will be maligned.

The evangelist must be patient, long suffering and not get discouraged. He must have tact and a willingness to be cool without compromising. At times discouragement and dissolution will give the evangelist second thoughts as to his call. THis is no time to quit.

SECTION FOUR

The Qualifications of the Evangelist

Much is said about the qualification of the elders as outlined in **I Timothy 3:1-7** and **Titus 1:5-9**. Yet, very little is ever said or taught concerning the qualifications that a qualified evangelist should have.

- Faithfulness (**Tim. 1:5**), Paul, as he writes to Timothy, gives him this charge. "Now, the end of the commandment is love out of a pure heart, and a good conscience and faith unfeigned." Be thou an example of the believer in word, in conversation, in love, in spirit, in Faith, in purity." (**I Tim. 4:13**)

- Pure conscience (**I Tim. 1:5**). "Pure" denotes unmixed conscience, testimony from within.

- Nourished up in the faith (**I Tim. 4:6**). "...Thou shalt be a good minister...nourished up in the words of faith and of good doctrine..." As the evangelist continues to instruct, he must study, administer therapy, being nourished up in the faith.

- Be an example (**I Tim. 4:12**). "...But be thou an example..." The evangelist must not let anyone look down on him, but he must be a pattern or mold for the believers to imitate and reproduce in their lives.

- Take heed to self and doctrine (**I Time. 4:16**) "Take heed unto thyself and unto the doctrine..." Holy living and sound doctrine go together. If the evangelist wishes to have salvation, his profession and teaching must be in harmony.

- Pure (**I Tim. 5:22**) "...Keep thyself pure." The evangelist must keep himself in full conformity with God's moral and spiritual laws with regard to selecting and ordaining elders and in any other matter.

- Teach and Exhort (**I Tim. 6:12**) "...these things teach and exhort." He must have the ability to instruct and motivate.

- Godly (**I Tim.6:2**) "...and follow after righteousness..." This means to practice that which is right.

- Bold (**II Tim 1:7**) "For God has not given us the spirit of fear but of power and of love and of sound mind.

- Endure affliction and hardships (**II Tim. 1:8-12, 2:3**). "But be thou partaker of the affliction of the gospel according to the power to God." 'Thou therefore endure hardness as a good soldier of Jesus Christ." Why? "Yea, and all that live godly in Christ shall suffer persecution." (**II Tim. 3:12**)

- Must be understanding (**II Tim. 2:7**)" ...and the Lord gives understanding in all things." An evangelist must put his mind to work; mere reading will not get the job done!

- Studious (**II Tim. 2:15**) "Study to show thyself approved unto God, a workman that need not be ashamed, rightly dividing the word of truth." The evangelist must be a serious student of the word of God if he is to lead, guide and interpret the word of God.

- Not quarrelsome (**II Tim. 2:24**) "And the servant of the Lord must not strive." If the evangelist is to be successful, he cannot be one that is contentious.

- Meek (**2 Tim 2:25**)"...in meekness instructing those that opposes themselves..." The evangelist must be in possession of a mild inner attitude and disposition.

- Know the scriptures. (**2 Tim. 3:15**) "And that from a babe has known the scripture..." The evangelist must not just merely know about the scriptures, he must know the scriptures!

- Rebuke sin. (**2 Tim 4:2**) "Preach the word...reprove, rebuke..." The evangelist must point out sin, and condemn it in the strongest way possible.

- Not vengeful. (**2 Tim 4:14**) "The evangelist must let the Lord give out punishment." He must let God exact revenge.

- Speak sound words. (**Tit. 2:1**) "But speak thou the things which become sound doctrine." The words of the evangelist must be from God's word, the Bible; they must ring with the authority of Heaven and they must be health giving to his hearers.

When a congregation acts out to hire an evangelist, careful consideration should be given to their qualifications as well as those that are normally associated with the evangelist: good speaker, good organizer, good mixture, good reputation and the fact "is he married?"

SECTION FIVE

The Evangelist's Spiritual Life

More often than not the evangelist is faced with discouragement. This Neurosis is often the killer of dreams, and the bringer of depression and guilt complexes. Too many evangelists suffer from spiritual burnout. This affects their total life! Family life suffers; children are abused and neglected. Evangelists contemplate suicide, running away from home and responsibility. Others not only have to leave the ministry but they also leave the faith. 'They lose sight of their objective because those that they serve have pumped them dry. They become shadows of the person who started out with such faith, full of dreams, ideologies, and a fervent spirit! They are like rusted out automobiles that once held great promises of longevity and wear, but now are nothing more than dinosaur of the past.

Sometimes the frustration and depression of the ministry can be traced back to the evangelist's study habits. Most evangelists will spend time studying to fortify others, instruct others and try to find solutions to their everyday problems. But very seldom do they study for themselves, very seldom do they spend time in the word of God for their own spiritual benefit. Many evangelists become all periphery and no center; all spokes and no hub; a car without an engine; clouds without rain. Many an evangelist has become like the Disciples of Christ in **Luke 9:13-17.** When they saw the multitudes surrounding them, they came to Jesus and asked him to "send the multitudes away." When the ministry becomes a burden, when people become a burden, they feel like sending the multitudes away. But Jesus does not heed their request, he tells them to feed the multitude, **(13),** and feed them He does. The point is you cannot send the multitudes away, you still have to give and keep on giving, and the only possible way for this to happen is for the evangelist to keep his well filled! He needs to overflow with the spiritual waters of God's word if he is to be able to keep giving, even when he may not want to.

How then does the evangelist keep his battery filled? First of all, he needs to develop a strong and healthy relationship with God through a daily devotional, extensive Bible study, meditation, and relaxation.

Every Christian should fortify himself every day with

God's word for his own personal edification. The Psalmist David said it this way, "I will instruct thee and teach thee in the way which thou shalt go; I will guide thee with mine eyes." **(Psalms 32:8)** David knew that his internal fortitude came from God! Therefore, he knew he needed to know the word of God. In **Psalms 119:11**, he said, "Thy word have I hid in mine heart, that I may not sin against thee." It is through the indwelling word that God gives power to his servant." If the evangelist wants to be an effective tool for the Master, if he wants **John 7:39** to be a reality in his life, then he must, and I underline the word *must*, spend time in daily contact with the word of God himself!

One must realize that it is in the solitude of this personal inner chamber that the word of God recreates that new heart. The evangelist, as he spends time in his devotional study, will find that he cannot, "regard iniquity in his heart for the Lord will not hear him" **(Ps. 66:18)** God will show him through his word that the "sacrifices of God are a broken spirit: a broken and contrite heart," God will not despise. It is in this daily devotional that God's word recreated that new man. No evangelist can be fresh and invigorating whom does not spend time in daily communication with God. God's line of communication is only through his word; therefore, the evangelist needs to meditate upon it. **(Ps.1)**

In his devotional life, the evangelist must also imitate the

Master in regards to his prayer life. In **Mark 1:35**, we have recorded by the Spirit the habit of the early prayer life of Christ, "and in the morning, rising upon a great while before day, he went out, and departed into a solitary place and there prayed." The evangelist should begin each day with a diligent prayer. His daily life should also include time that is set aside to offer prayers throughout the day. On occasions he may find himself having to leave the multitudes and go off to the solitude of the mountains to pray. (**Mk. 6:46**) It may be that the evangelist may have to do even as the master, "...that He went out into a mountain to pray and continued all night in prayer to God." (**Lk.6:12**) It is obvious that Jesus, on numerous occasions, had to desert the crowds in order to be alone in the wilderness to pray. (**Lk. 5:16**) The evangelist needs, then, to be a man of prayer. He leads the congregation in this aspect (**I Tim. 2:1-8**). The evangelist should lead the church in prayers for:

- Those in places of high authority (**vs. 2**)
- The purpose for this is two-fold
  - ○ That the church may live in peace (**vs. 2b**)
  - ○ The salvation of the world (**vs. 4**)
- Qualifications of those who pray
  - ○ Through the meditation of Christ (**vs. 5**)
  - ○ And lives that are holy (**vs. 8**)
- Types of prayers that should be uttered (**vs. 1**)

- Supplications, petitions for the fulfillment of certain definite needs which are keenly felt
- Prayers, general in meaning, and are used to convey every form of reverent address to Deity
- Intercession, pleading in the interest of others, without holding back in any form.
- Giving of thanks, the giving of gratitude for these men in high authority

It would do well to remember that all of God's great servants were men of tremendous prayer and if one is to follow in the steps of these gladiators, one must possess this characteristic.

Extensive Bible Study

Every evangelist knows that last Sunday's room raiser is past history, and another roof raiser must be built for this upcoming Sunday. Therefore, every evangelist must spend time in an intensified course of Bible study. It was said of the late Gus Nichols that he began his day with "two hours of Bible reading, two hours of studying Bible references, and one hour of meditation." Every evangelist should have time to study every day some portion of the Scriptures, some particular subject, some current issue that may need to be addressed or one that seems to be lurking in the not too distant future.

Someone has said that the evangelist should spend "one hour in preparation for every minute he speaks," I don't know the reality of this but it would be sound advice to follow.

One thing that two to four hours of daily disciplined study will do is that the evangelist will never run out of substance to preach on, but rather will never have the time to preach all that he needs and wants to preach.

In this period of extensive Bible study, there should be time that is set aside to meditate and to contemplate over that which has been studied and digested. It is in reality here where what has been read and what has been studied is learned.

Relaxation

Evangelists must realize that every time they preach they exert a tremendous amount of energy. Sooner or later this tremendous exercise begins to take its effect on the body, the mind, and the emotions. Therefore, the evangelist needs to have some form of outlet, whether it be walking, jogging, racquetball or swimming. Every evangelist should have at least one day a week where he can relax, do something other than those things which are related to the rigors and pressures of the ministry. The evangelist should remember that each time he mounts the pulpit and speaks for forty-five minutes, he is doing the equivalent of eight hours of manual labor. When he does this two times on Sunday, he has expended some sixteen-man hours. Even Jesus had the need to spend time with his disciples in rest (**Mk 6:31**).

Secondly, the evangelist needs to watch his diet! As one who has to battle with the bulge, his diet will invariably affect his stamina, productivity and leadership, As a matter of fact; it may shorten his life. I read a statistic that came across my desk; now I cannot vouch for its validity, but it said, "that the life expectancy of a minister on the average was forty-six years of age." When you look at the pressure cooker that the average evangelist is under: sermon, preparation, administration, leadership development, counseling, discipline training and disciplining, he had better watch his health or he will not be around to enjoy the fruits of his labor. Thirdly, and not the third in essence of importance which has an impact on the spiritual life of the evangelist, of the list, is the amount of time he spends with his wife and children. Every evangelist whose wife is not a part of his daily ministry needs to spend some portion of the day in contact with his wife - through Bible study, prayer, meditation, and in exhortation. Some time should be spent during the week separate and apart from the family time with each other, whether it is but for a sandwich or a walk in the mall. Maybe a movie or a walk in the park, or get away weekends or days should be part of the agenda.

An evangelist needs to make time for his children and spend that quality time with them. He needs to be available for them as well as for the church. What affects them affects him. What affects him will affect his ministry. Therefore, he needs to spend some time every day or week with his children.

The evangelist must recognize that he is not the only one under the pressures of the ministry, but that his wife and children are under the constant gaze of unkind and inconsiderate members who believe that the wife and children of the evangelist are born perfect and without fault. They are measured in terms of dress, conduct, manners and involvement. His children cannot act or grow up like normal children, and this brings about resentment from his offspring, which can lead to disaster for the evangelist. The wise, evangelist will seek to protect his family from undue pressures and hostilities from the membership. Also, when he deals with his wife and children, he needs to remember that he is also husband and father first, then evangelist! If not, much of what he may accomplish may be destroyed by the unchristian attitude that his wife and children may develop.

CONCLUSION

The work of an evangelist is a most demanding one. Therefore, it requires the greatest dedication from those who would do the work. To this end Paul gives this charge: "but the end of the charge is love out of a pure heart and a good conscience and faith unfeigned." **(I Timothy 1:5)** This charge is needed today for all of God's servant. He must love the lost as well as those whom God's Word has rescued. This love, active good will, comes from a heart that is unmixed in its motives. To this end the evangelist must, endeavor to know the gospel which he proclaims. He should proclaim it with fervency and enthusiasm, remembering that he is God's spokesman to his people. Therefore God's evangelist should make sure that before he mounts the pulpit that he has spent time in the closets of his study and should not leave until he has been infused and comes out overflowing with God's message to the church.

No evangelist should administrate the church whose conscience is not good. The conscience of a man is that inner knowledge that helps one to know oneself. The evangelist must know within himself that the doctrine he proclaims, the manner in which he trains the church in the development of preachers, elders, deacons, teachers is in accordance with the revealed truth of God. He must know within himself that in the setting in order of the church, that he must establish the right pattern of worship. That the mission of evangelism both within the local and foreign field be carried out. That the church glorifies God in its benevolent work and that there is the establishment of the proper atmosphere for the development of God's pre-ordained leaders.

No evangelist can fulfill his responsibility of defending the faith without a "pure conscience." To this end the administrator of God must spend time in profound study of doctrinal and current events. His library should be replenished from time to time with materials that will further his knowledge of the truth and allow him to stand firm and without any reservations at all, his prayer life must be one that denotes a positive awareness of his relationship with God and that there is not guilt in his approach to God's throne of mercy.

Another area that calls for both "love and a good conscience" is in the area of disciplining the church. Here the administrator must have a proper balance. His duty in disciplining the church should stem from his love of God, his word and the soul of the person. This will generally result in the restoration of the delinquent when care and concern are shown.

The last part of Paul's charge deals and summarizes the qualifications of the administrator, "faith unfeigned." The administrator must be a man of profound faith. One who has deep-rooted trust and confidence in the Son of God and the word of God. He must have confidence that he is God's administrator and will act based on that "unhypocritical faith." When things are tough and it seems like all is useless, it will be his faith in the promise of God that will sustain him. This charge of "Pure love, conscience and faith" is the corner stone of the church administrator. It is this that will help him to achieve the lofty goal of those who have been called to perform the most noble call upon the shores of time.

If this treatise helps anyone to know and to fulfill his ministry the objective of its writer will have been accomplished. May God's richest blessings be upon all those who seek to administrate the church of our Lord!

BIBLIOGRAPHY

Acthemeir, Elizabeth, *Creative Preaching Finding the Word.* Abingdon Press, Nashville, Tenn., 1981.

Aycock, Don M., *Preaching with Power and Purpose*, Mercer University Press, 1982

Barclay, Willliam, *The Letters to Timothy, Titus and Philemon*, Westminister Press, Philadelphia, Penn. 1960.

Barnes, Alford, *Thessalonians, Timothy, Titus and Philemon*, Baker Book House, Grand Rapids, Michigan, 1949.

Bartlett, Gene E., *The Audacity of Preaching*, Harper and Brothers, New York, New York, 1961.

Biblical Illustrator, Baker Book House, Grand Rapids, Michigan, Vol.20.

Blackwood, A. W., *The Fine Art of Preaching*, Baker Book House, Grand Rapids, Michigan, 1978.

Claypool, John R., *The Preaching Event*, Word Books, Waco, Texas, 1980.

Dewelt, D. M., *Paul's Letters to Timothy, Titus and Philemon*, college Press, Joplin, Missouri, 1979.

Fant, Clyde E. *Preaching for Today*, Harper and Row, Publishers, N.Y., 1975.

Haselden, Kyle, *The Urgency of Preaching*, Harper and Row, New York, New York, 1963.

Hendricksen, William, *Thessalonians Timothy and Titus*. Baker Book House, Grand Rapids, Michigan, 1983.

Ironside, H.A., *Timothy Titus, Philemon*. Loizeau Brothers, Neptune, New Jersey, 1947.

Gibbs, Alfred, *The Preacher and His Preaching*, Walterick Publishers, Kansas City, Kansas, 1939.

Massey, James E., *Designing the Sermon*, Abingdon Press, Nashville, Tenn. 1981.

Meyers, Jack, *The Preacher and His Work*, Lambert Book House, 1960.

North, Stafford, *Preaching Man and Method*, OCC Publishers, Oklahoma City, Oklahoma, 1977.

Noyes, Morgan, Phelps, *Preaching the Word of God*, Charles Scribner's and Sons, 1943.

Robertson, A. T., *Word Pictures in the N.T.*, Baker Book House, Grand Rapids, Michigan, 1978.

Spence, H.D.M., Exell, Joseph's, *The Pulpit Commentary* Vol. 21, Wm. B. Eerdmans, Pub. Grand Rapids, Michigan, 1978.

Stott, John R. W., *Preaching with Power and Purpose*. Mercer University Press, 1982.

Vincent, Marvin R., *Word Studies in the New Testament*, Vol. IV., Macdonald Publishers Co. McLean, Virginia.

Wiershe, W.B., *Be Faithful*, Victor Book House, Wheaton, IL. 1982.

CPSIA information can be obtained
at www.ICGtesting.com
Printed in the USA
BVHW071658120620
581245BV00003B/105